P IS FOR PUPS!

A PAW Patrol Visual Dictionary

How to Use Your Dictionary

Letter

Each page of this dictionary has words that start with a different letter! These pages are in the order of the alphabet.

A B C D
E F G H
I J K L
M N O
P Q R S
T U V W
X Y Z

This is the whole alphabet!

The words on each page are in the order of the alphabet, too!

Every word has a picture and a sentence explaining what it means!

A

airplane

An **airplane** is a machine with an engine that has wings and can fly through the air!

alligator

An **alligator** is a big reptile with strong jaws, big teeth, and a long tail.

anchor

An **anchor** is a heavy object attached to a rope or chain. Anchors are used to keep boats in place.

There's an anchor on my badge!

apple

An **apple** is a type of fruit that grows on trees.

autumn

Autumn is another word for "fall," the season between summer and winter.

backpack

A **backpack** is a bag that goes over your shoulders and sits on your back. It's used to carry things like school supplies or camping gear.

bandage

A **bandage** covers up a cut or scrape so it can heal.

Bandages help keep out germs!

beach

A **beach** is the place where a body of water meets the land!

bicycle

A **bicycle** is a two-wheeled vehicle. You ride it by pushing on the pedals with your feet.

book

A **book** is a printed work made up of pages and bound by a cover. You're reading one!

C

car

A **car** is a vehicle with four wheels and an engine.

caterpillar

A **caterpillar** is an insect! It wraps itself in a cocoon then turns into a butterfly.

costume

A **costume** is a special outfit that makes you look like someone or something else.

My Halloween costume makes me look like a vampire!

crayon

A **crayon** is a stick of colored wax used for writing and drawing.

cupcake

A **cupcake** is a small, sweet, baked good made with flour, sugar, and eggs.

dancer

A **dancer** is someone who moves rhythmically to music.

dinosaur

A **dinosaur** is a reptile that lived on Earth millions of years ago.

doctor

A **doctor** is someone who treats sick and injured people.

A doctor keeps you healthy!

doll

A **doll** is a toy that looks like a person.

dump truck

A **dump truck** is a truck used to carry loose material such as sand, dirt, and gravel.

E

ear

An **ear** is a body part that helps you hear.

eat

To **eat** means to chew and swallow food.

egg

An **egg** is an oval container made of shell. Eggs hold some baby animals such as birds, snakes, and turtles, until they are ready to be born.

elephant

An **elephant** is a big animal with large ears and a long nose called a trunk.

envelope

An **envelope** is a flat, paper container with a sealable flap used to mail a letter.

A group of elephants is called a herd!

face

Your **face** is on the front of your head. It includes your nose, mouth, and eyes!

farm

A **farm** is an area of land that grows plants and raises animals!

My farm has pumpkins, cows, and pigs!

firefighter

A **firefighter** is someone who puts out fires.

flute

A **flute** is an instrument shaped like a long tube that you blow air into to make music.

football

A **football** is a leather, oval-shaped ball filled with air.

G garage

A **garage** is a building or shed where people park their car.

gift

A **gift** is a surprise that you make or buy for someone else. We give gifts on special occasions like birthdays!

I love giving gifts!

glue

Glue is a gooey substance that is used for sticking objects together.

grapes

Grapes are a really yummy fruit that grows on vines.

guitar

A **guitar** is an instrument with six or 12 strings.

hat

A **hat** is an accessory you wear on your head.

horse

A **horse** is an animal with long legs, a tail, hooves and hair on its neck called a mane.

house

A **house** is a building where people live.

husky

A **Husky** is a dog that's good at pulling sleds.

I'm a Husky!

hydrant

A **hydrant** is a metal object on a street. Firefighters connect their hoses to hydrants to get water!

I

ice cream

Ice cream is a cold, sweet dessert made from cream and sugar.

Ice cream is delicious!

igloo

An **igloo** is a house made out of ice.

iguana

An **iguana** is a kind of lizard originally from Latin America.

iris

The **iris** is the colored part of your eye.

iron

An **iron** is a triangle-shaped device that heats up in order to smooth out the wrinkles in clothes.

jack-o-lantern

A **jack-o-lantern** is a carved pumpkin.

People make jack-o-lanterns for Halloween!

jam

Jam is a spread made by cooking fruit and sugar together.

jewelry

Jewelry is the word for things people wear to decorate themselves. Necklaces, rings, bracelets, and earrings are all jewelry.

joey

A **joey** is a baby kangaroo!

juice

Juice is the liquid that is squeezed from fruits and vegetables.

 **kazoo**

A **kazoo** is an instrument that you hum into.

key

A **key** is a metal object that is used to open a lock.

 **kid**

A **kid** is a young person—or a young goat!

kite

A **kite** is a toy made of wood, paper, and string that flies in the wind.

kitten

A **kitten** is a young cat.

Kittens are super cute!

ladybug

A **ladybug** is a small red or yellow beetle with black spots.

lava

Lava is hot, melted rock that comes out of volcanoes.

Volcano Island sometimes has lava!

lemon

A **lemon** is a yellow oval citrus fruit with very tart juice.

lighthouse

A **lighthouse** sits on the shore and shines bright to guide ships at sea.

lunch

Lunch is a meal you eat in the middle of the day.

meow

Meow is the sound a cat makes.

Cali meows all the time!

money

Money is coins or bills used to buy things.

mother

A **mother** is a female parent.

mouse

A **mouse** is a very small animal with whiskers and a long tail.

music

If you play an instrument or sing a song, you're making **music!**

nap

A **nap** is a short rest during the day.

necktie

A **necktie** is an accessory that goes around your neck.

nest

Birds build **nests** and lay their eggs inside of them.

number

Numbers are the units used for counting. Numbers show "how many" or "how much."

nurse

A **nurse** helps take care of sick or hurt people.

Nurses work at schools and hospitals!

o octopus

An **octopus** is a sea creature with eight arms.

orange

An **orange** is a tasty fruit.

Orange is the color of my helmet, vest, and hovercraft, too!

origami

Origami is the Japanese art of folding paper into special shapes like birds or flowers.

ostrich

Ostriches are the biggest birds. They can run really fast!

over

Over is the opposite of under. This horse is jumping over a hurdle!

pajamas

Pajamas are what you wear to bed.

picture

A **picture** is something you draw or paint.

pirate

Pirates were adventurers who sailed the seven seas!

It's fun to pretend to be a pirate!

porthole

A **porthole** is a window in a boat or ship.

puppy

A **puppy** is a young dog.

Q

quack

A **quack** is the sound a duck makes.

quarter

A **quarter** is a coin worth 25 cents.

queen

A **queen** is a female ruler of a country.

quiet

If you're **quiet**, you're not making any noise.

Super spies have to be super quiet!

quilt

A **quilt** is a kind of blanket.

rainbow

A **rainbow** is an arch of colors that forms in the sky.

recycle

When you **recycle** something, you're re-using it instead of throwing it out!

river

A **river** is a large stream of water.

Ready, set, get wet!

road

A **road** is what people drive or ride bikes on.

rooster

A **rooster** is a male chicken.

sandcastle

A **sandcastle** is a structure made out of sand. You can build sandcastles at the beach!

snowflake

A **snowflake** is a feathery ice crystal that forms when it's cold outside.

soccer ball

A **soccer ball** is a black and white inflated ball.

spider

A **spider** is an eight-legged creature that spins webs.

I see a lot of spiders in the jungle!

star

Stars shine bright in the night sky.

tail

A **tail** is the rear part of some animals. Dogs and monkeys have tails!

toy

A **toy** is an object that you play with.

tractor

A **tractor** is a big machine used on farms.

tricycle

A **tricycle** is a vehicle with pedals and three wheels.

Lots of kids have tricycles... like me!

turtle

A **turtle** is a reptile with a hard shell.

ukulele

A **ukulele** is a small string instrument.

umbrella

An **umbrella** is a round piece of cloth on a handle that keeps you dry in the rain.

under

Under is the opposite of over. Fish swim under water.

unicycle

A **unicycle** is a vehicle with two pedals and only one wheel!

upside down

If something is **upside down**, the top is where the bottom usually is.

I love to flip upside down!

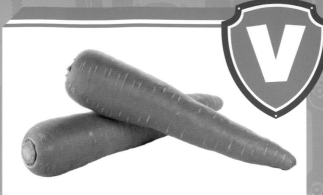

vacuum cleaner

A **vacuum cleaner** is a machine that sucks up dirt and dust.

vegetable

A **vegetable** is the edible part of a plant, like a carrot or pepper.

vehicle

A **vehicle** is a machine that moves people (and pups!) from one place to another.

My digger is a vehicle!

vest

A **vest** is a jacket without sleeves.

violin

A **violin** is a stringed instrument played with a bow.

wallet

A **wallet** is a pocket-sized, folding holder for money.

watermelon

A **watermelon** is a large delicious fruit that's green on the outside and red on the inside.

week

There are seven days in one **week.**

Monday, Tuesday, Wednesday, Thursday, Friday, Saturday, Sunday!

windmill

A **windmill** turns the wind into power!

window

A **window** is a glass opening in a wall or vehicle that lets in air and light.

xenops

A **xenops** is a small kind of bird from Latin America.

Lots of words that start with x are said with a "z" sound, like xenops (zee-nops) and xylophone (zy-low-fone).

xylophone

A **xylophone** is a musical instrument made of narrow strips of metal or wood. Each strip makes a different sound!

x-ray

An **X-ray** is a photograph of the bones inside a person or animal's body.

I take X-rays of your bones to make sure everything is OK!

Y yard

A **yard** is the ground immediately outside a building. Lots of houses have front and backyards.

yell

If you're talking really loud, you're **yelling**.

yoga

Yoga is a form of exercise where people stretch and stand in special poses.

Yoga can be very relaxing!

yogurt

Yogurt is a creamy food made from milk.

yo-yo

A **yo-yo** is a toy that goes up and down on a string.

zebra

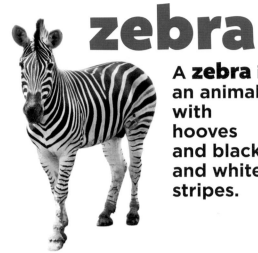

A **zebra** is an animal with hooves and black and white stripes.

zeppelin

A **zeppelin** is a large airship that travels through the sky.

zigzag

A **zigzag** is a line that goes back and forth.

zipline

A **zipline** is a rope or cable with a handle or harness for a rider to slide down.

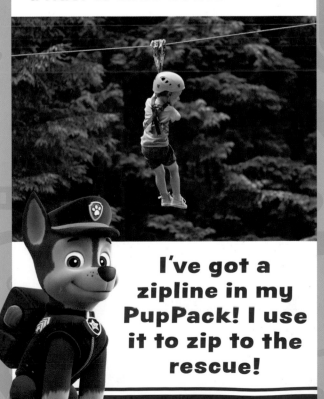

zipper

A **zipper** is a device that closes things like pants, backpacks, and purses.

I've got a zipline in my PupPack! I use it to zip to the rescue!

PAW Patrol

is on a
READING
ROLL!

Media Lab Books
For inquiries, call 646-838-6637

Copyright 2017 Topix Media Lab

Published by Topix Media Lab
14 Wall Street, Suite 4B
New York, NY 10005

Printed in China

ISBN-10: 1-942556-93-4
ISBN-13: 978-1-942556-93-0

1C 117 1